Samuel French Acting Edition

The Problem

by A.R. Gurney

SAMUELFRENCH.COM   SAMUELFRENCH.CO.UK

Copyright © 1968, 1996 by A.R. Gurney
All Rights Reserved

THE PROBLEM is fully protected under the copyright laws of the United States of America, the British Commonwealth, including Canada, and all other countries of the Copyright Union. All rights, including professional and amateur stage productions, recitation, lecturing, public reading, motion picture, radio broadcasting, television and the rights of translation into foreign languages are strictly reserved.

ISBN 978-0-573-62418-6

www.SamuelFrench.com
www.SamuelFrench.co.uk

For Production Enquiries

United States and Canada
Info@SamuelFrench.com
1-866-598-8449

United Kingdom and Europe
Plays@SamuelFrench.co.uk
020-7255-4302

Each title is subject to availability from Samuel French, depending upon country of performance. Please be aware that *THE PROBLEM* may not be licensed by Samuel French in your territory. Professional and amateur producers should contact the nearest Samuel French office or licensing partner to verify availability.

CAUTION: Professional and amateur producers are hereby warned that *THE PROBLEM* is subject to a licensing fee. Publication of this play(s) does not imply availability for performance. Both amateurs and professionals considering a production are strongly advised to apply to Samuel French before starting rehearsals, advertising, or booking a theatre. A licensing fee must be paid whether the title(s) is presented for charity or gain and whether or not admission is charged. Professional/Stock licensing fees are quoted upon application to Samuel French.

No one shall make any changes in this title(s) for the purpose of production. No part of this book may be reproduced, stored in a retrieval system, or transmitted in any form, by any means, now known or yet to be invented, including mechanical, electronic, photocopying, recording, videotaping, or otherwise, without the prior written permission of the publisher. No one shall upload this title(s), or part of this title(s), to any social media websites.

For all enquiries regarding motion picture, television, and other media rights, please contact Samuel French.

MUSIC USE NOTE

Licensees are solely responsible for obtaining formal written permission from copyright owners to use copyrighted music in the performance of this play and are strongly cautioned to do so. If no such permission is obtained by the licensee, then the licensee must use only original music that the licensee owns and controls. Licensees are solely responsible and liable for all music clearances and shall indemnify the copyright owners of the play(s) and their licensing agent, Samuel French, against any costs, expenses, losses and liabilities arising from the use of music by licensees. Please contact the appropriate music licensing authority in your territory for the rights to any incidental music.

IMPORTANT BILLING AND CREDIT REQUIREMENTS

If you have obtained performance rights to this title, please refer to your licensing agreement for important billing and credit requirements.

CAST OF CHARACTERS

THE HUSBAND, *in his thirties.*
THE WIFE, *also in her thirties.*

(As simple a set as possible: the suggestion of a study. A leather chair with a matching footstool, a reading light behind it. A bookcase.)

The Problem

At curtain, the HUSBAND *is sitting in the chair, feet up on the footstool, reading a book, smoking a pipe, taking notes into a notebook comfortably propped on his knee. After a moment, the* WIFE *comes in from the* L., *hugely pregnant. She stands looking at him. He continues to read.*

WIFE. Hey.
HUSBAND. (*Not looking at her.*) I'm reading, dear.
WIFE. (*Sticking out her stomach.*) I know. But look at me.
HUSBAND. (*Still reading.*) I'm preparing for a class, dear.
WIFE. I know, but just look. (*She crosses to him, stands by his chair, and sticks out her stomach.*) Just take a gander.
HUSBAND. (*Turns his head and looks right into her stomach. He starts, takes off his glasses, looks again, and then looks up into her face.*) Well, well.
WIFE. Yes.
HUSBAND. Surprise, surprise.
WIFE. Yes.
HUSBAND. Merry Christmas.
WIFE. Exactly. (*Pause.*)
HUSBAND. Why have I never noticed before?
WIFE. Because I wear loose-fitting clothes.
HUSBAND. That's true.
WIFE. Clothes without waists. Merri-mekkos. Sack dresses. Granny gowns.
HUSBAND. That's true.
WIFE. Large, shapeless flannel nightgowns.
HUSBAND. True enough.

WIFE. So only now, tonight, does it seem to show.

HUSBAND. I see. (*Pause. They smile at each other. Then he looks at his watch.*) I've got to teach a class in an hour.

WIFE. Oh, I know. And I've got to go out to a meeting on Open Housing.

HUSBAND. So . . .

WIFE. I just wanted you to know. (*Pause.*) So you could plan.

HUSBAND. Yes. I will. I'll plan accordingly. (*Smiles at her again, puts on his glasses, and returns to his book. She starts off L., and then stops.*)

WIFE. Oh, there's one thing, though.

HUSBAND. (*Reading.*) Mmmmmm?

WIFE. One small problem.

HUSBAND. (*Reading.*) Mmmmm. And what's that, dear?

WIFE. I don't know whether you've thought about this, or not.

HUSBAND. (*Looking up.*) State the problem. And I'll tell you whether I've thought about it.

WIFE. It's a little tricky.

HUSBAND. Well. We're married, after all.

WIFE. Yes. That's why it's a little tricky.

HUSBAND. Perhaps. But that's also why you should feel free to speak out.

WIFE. All right. (*Pause.*) You see, I'm not absolutely sure that this . . . (*She looks down at her stomach.*) is yours. (*Pause. He marks his place in his book, puts it down carefully, takes off his glasses, and then looks up.*)

HUSBAND. Ah. So that's the problem.

WIFE. Yes. That's the problem.

HUSBAND. I think I'll trust you on this one, dear.

WIFE. That's sweet of you, darling. (*Pause.*) But do I trust myself?

HUSBAND. I think you should. So there we are.

WIFE. But . . .

THE PROBLEM

HUSBAND. But what?

WIFE. The thing is . . . Now how do I put this?

HUSBAND. Speak frankly now.

WIFE. I'll try. The thing is . . . that you and I . . . haven't made love very much. Recently.

HUSBAND. Is that true?

WIFE. I think it is. Not very much. Not recently.

HUSBAND. Hmmm. Define "recently."

WIFE. Well, I mean . . . five years, more or less . . . give or take a month or two.

HUSBAND. Is that true?

WIFE. I think it is. (*Pause.*)

HUSBAND. (*Lighting his pipe.*) My gosh, has it been that long?

WIFE. Oh, yes.

HUSBAND. Well, well. And so . . .

WIFE. And so . . .

HUSBAND. And so you mind, obviously.

WIFE. Mind?

HUSBAND. Mind that we haven't. Much. Recently.

WIFE. Oh, no. Oh, no, no. I don't *mind*. Why should I *mind?*

HUSBAND. Well, then . . .

WIFE. (*Pointing to her stomach.*) I'm just thinking of *this,* that's all.

HUSBAND. Oh, I *see!*

WIFE. (*Smiling.*) You see?

HUSBAND. Of *course.* I see the con*nec*tion! (*He slaps his head.*) For*give* me. I was thinking about my class.

WIFE. Oh, heavens. I forgive you. You love your work.

HUSBAND. Yes, but I'm with you now. I'm on your wave length now.

WIFE. Oh, good.

HUSBAND. Yes, yes. I understand now. What you're really saying is . . . now stop me if I'm wrong . . . but what you're really saying is that you think someone else might have impregnated you.

WIFE. More or less. Yes.
HUSBAND. I see, I see, I see.
WIFE. It's possible, after all.
HUSBAND. Yes. It's possible.
WIFE. On these evenings that you have to go teach.
HUSBAND. Yes. When you go out to your meetings.
WIFE. Yes. Exactly.
HUSBAND. So we do have a problem there, don't we?
WIFE. Yes. We really do.

(*Pause; he looks at her, looks at her stomach, scratches his head, taps his teeth with a pencil, lights his pipe, twirls his glasses.*)

HUSBAND. You know, darling . . . it occurs to me . . . that I should have made love to you more.
WIFE. Oh, no, no. . . .
HUSBAND. I'm kicking myself now.
WIFE. Oh, don't, don't. . . .
HUSBAND. I am. Things would have been much simpler.
WIFE. Oh, sweetheart, stop punishing yourself.
HUSBAND. But why didn't I? Darn it! Darn it all!
WIFE. Darling, you have your work.
HUSBAND. Oh, sure, but . . .
WIFE. You have your intellectual life . . .
HUSBAND. That's all very well, but . . .
WIFE. You had your book to get out . . .
HUSBAND. Yes, yes, but, darling, that doesn't really answer the question. The question is, why haven't I made love to you in the past five years? That's the question.

(*Pause.*)

WIFE. Well. You used to laugh too much, maybe.
HUSBAND. Laugh?
WIFE. Yes. In the old days. Whenever we started to make love, you'd start to chuckle.

THE PROBLEM

HUSBAND. I did, didn't I? I remember now. (*He chuckles.*)

WIFE. Yes. You'd chuckle.

HUSBAND. (*Chuckling.*) Because the whole thing struck me as being slightly absurd. (*Chuckling.*) When you think about it. (*Chuckling.*) I should learn to control myself. (*He chuckles louder; controls himself stoically; then bursts into loud laughter; then forces himself to subside; looks at her.*) I'm sorry.

WIFE. Oh, don't be sorry. I was just as bad.

HUSBAND. Did you chuckle?

WIFE. No. Actually I'd cry.

HUSBAND. I don't remember your crying.

WIFE. Well, I'd whimper.

HUSBAND. Yes, yes! You would. You'd whimper. (*Chuckles.*)

WIFE. Well, I felt so sad! Making love. While all these horrible things are going on in the world.

HUSBAND. Yes. So you'd whimper. I remember now.

WIFE. Viet Nam . . . Urban blight . . . all that. . . . I felt so guilty!

HUSBAND. And I felt so absurd.

WIFE. Yes. You chuckling, me whimpering. . . .

HUSBAND. Yes. Oh, yes.

WIFE. And so it wasn't very conducive.

HUSBAND. Right. So we gave it up. That answers that. (*Pause; picks up his book and starts to read.*)

WIFE. But now there's this. (*Indicates her stomach.*)

HUSBAND. (*Reading; taking notes.*) Keep it.

WIFE. What?

HUSBAND. Keep it. Bear it. Bring it home.

WIFE. Oh, darling. . . .

HUSBAND. Give it my name. Consider me its father.

WIFE. Oh, sweetheart.

HUSBAND. I've let you down. Now I'll make it up. Keep it.

WIFE. But I'm partly to blame.

HUSBAND. But I'm the man.

THE PROBLEM

WIFE. You certainly are! You certainly are the man!
HUSBAND. And now I'm afraid that I must prepare for my class.
WIFE. Yes. And I've got to go to my meeting.

(*They smile at each other; then she starts out* L.; *then she stops, and stands reflectively. After a moment, he looks at her.*)

HUSBAND. But you're not satisfied.
WIFE. Oh, I am, I am.
HUSBAND. Darling, we've been married ten years. You are not satisfied.
WIFE. You've got a class.
HUSBAND. My wife comes first. Come on. What's the problem now?
WIFE. I'm embarrassed even to bring it up.
HUSBAND. (*Tenderly.*) Come on. Out with it. Tell Daddy.
WIFE. All right. (*Pause.*) What if this . . . (*She looks at her stomach.*) turns out to be black?

(*Pause.*)

HUSBAND. Black?
WIFE. Black. Or at least mulatto. Depending on how the chromosomes line up.
HUSBAND. (*Pause. Lights his pipe again.*) Mmmmm.
WIFE. You see? You see the problem?
HUSBAND. (*Nodding.*) Mmmmm.
WIFE. I mean, can you still act as its father if it's black?
HUSBAND. (*Puffing away.*) Mmmmmm. (*Looks at her wryly.*) Yes, well, that puts a different complexion on things.
WIFE. (*Giggling.*) Funny.
HUSBAND. (*Chuckling.*) That's a horse of a different color.

THE PROBLEM

WIFE. (*Laughing.*) Now cut it out. You're awful. (*Stops laughing.*) Try to be serious.

HUSBAND. (*Pause. Settles down.*) Black, eh?

WIFE. I should have told you before.

HUSBAND. No, no. I should have assumed it.

WIFE. It just slipped my mind, I guess.

HUSBAND. I'm glad it did. That says something for America these days.

WIFE. Yes. But it's still a problem.

HUSBAND. In this case, yes. I'd say so. (*Pause.*) So you must let me think it out.

WIFE. But your class . . .

HUSBAND. I'll just be less prepared than I like to be. Which may be good. Which may be very good. Which may make things more lively and spontaneous. So let me think about this other problem. (*Puffs on his pipe; she stands watching him.*) I could still adopt it.

WIFE. How?

HUSBAND. We could tell the world that you had a blue baby. Which died. And then we could bring home the black one. Which we say we adopted.

WIFE. That sounds awfully complicated.

HUSBAND. I know it.

WIFE. Awfully baroque.

HUSBAND. I know it.

WIFE. Besides, the real father might object. He might take pride in it himself.

HUSBAND. Need he know?

WIFE. Oh, yes. Because he'll see it, after all.

HUSBAND. You mean, he'll continue to come around.

WIFE. Oh, yes. After I'm home from the hospital. And capable of sexual intercourse again.

HUSBAND. I see.

WIFE. So that pretty well puts a damper on the adopting idea.

HUSBAND. Yes, it does. (*He thinks.*)

WIFE. But you have your class . . .

HUSBAND. No, no. Now wait a minute. . . . (*He

thinks carefully, then suddenly pounds his fist on the arm of his chair.) Sweetheart, I'm going to be honest with you. (*Points to the footstool.*) Sit down.

WIFE. (*Looking at the footstool.*) I can't sit down. Your feet are there.

HUSBAND. I'll remove my feet. (*He does.*) Now sit down.

WIFE. All right. I'll sit down. (*Sits on the footstool in front of him.*)

HUSBAND. Now don't look at me. Face forward. Because this is going to be hard for me to tell, and hard for you to hear.

WIFE. All right. I won't look at you.

HUSBAND. And if I'm inarticulate about this, you must try to understand that this is a difficult thing for a man to tell his wife. I'm only doing it—I'm only telling you—because it seems to be the only way to solve this problem.

WIFE. (*Smoothing her skirt over her stomach.*) Yes. This problem.

HUSBAND. Now try not to interrupt, darling, unless you have to. Unless you're unclear about anything. Save your remarks and comments for the end. All right?

WIFE. I'll try.

HUSBAND. All right. (*He takes a deep breath.*) Now. To begin with, I've been lying to you this evening.

WIFE. Lying?

HUSBAND. Ssshhh. Lying. I don't have a class tonight. I've never had a class at night. I don't believe in evening classes. All these years I've been lying. The class that I've told you meets at night actually meets on Mondays, Wednesdays, and Fridays at 10 A.M.

WIFE. I see.

HUSBAND. You may well ask, therefore, where I go on these nights when I say I have classes. (*Pause.*) And that is what is so difficult to tell you. (*Pause.*) The fact is, I don't leave this house. Not really. Oh, I leave by the front door, all right. But I immediately circle around

THE PROBLEM

in back, and go down into the cellar by means of the bulkhead.

WIFE. I see.

HUSBAND. Now. What do I do in the cellar? You are probably asking yourself that. What do I do in the cellar? . . . Don't look at me, darling! (*Pause; then grimly.*) Here's what I do in the cellar. I make my way to a small space behind the furnace. And in that small space, I have hidden . . . certain things. (*Pause.*) What have I hidden? I'll tell you. (*He counts them off on his fingers.*) Some black theatrical make-up. A woolly wig. A complete change of clothes. And a small mirror. That's what I have hidden in the cellar.

WIFE. I see. . . .

HUSBAND. Yes. You see, my darling, or you're beginning to. When I go into the cellar, I set the mirror up on an adjacent waterpipe. I strip myself to the buff. I daub myself from head to toe with that dusky make-up. I glue on that curly wig. I don those makeshift clothes. I leave the cellar. Go to the front door. Ring the bell. And reappear to you. So you see, my poor darling, I am your Negro visitor, and have been all along.

WIFE. You.

HUSBAND. Me.

WIFE. But—

HUSBAND. Oh, I know it sounds implausible. But remember how you always lower the lights. Remember, too, that I played Othello in high school. Somehow I was able to pass. I have deceived you for these past years. Deceived my own wife! Disguising myself as a Negro, and capitalizing on the sympathies you naturally feel for that unhappy race!

WIFE. But . . . why?

HUSBAND. Because I wanted to make love to you. And somehow this seemed to be the only way I could do it. You'll have to admit it worked.

WIFE. (*Looking at her stomach.*) Oh, yes. It worked.

HUSBAND. So out of all this depravity, at least a child will be born. And I was its father, after all.

WIFE. I'm somewhat . . . stunned . . . by all this.

HUSBAND. I know you are, darling. (*Gets up.*) Try to assimilate it while I'm gone.

WIFE. Gone?

HUSBAND. I'm going down to the cellar now.

WIFE. To put on your costume?

HUSBAND. No. To burn it.

WIFE. Burn it?

HUSBAND. Yes. It's all over now. Because you know. The mask is off. Any attempt to wear it again would be foolish. I'd be nothing but a self-conscious amateur. Our love life would be as absurd as it was before I found this way around it. So I'm going to destroy my role. (*Pause; he looks at her.*) And when I come back, I want you gone.

WIFE. Gone?

HUSBAND. You must leave me now.

WIFE. No.

HUSBAND. You must. Oh, my darling, this urge to love you is still in me. I don't know what . . . oblique form . . . it will take next. Take the child and go.

WIFE. Never.

HUSBAND. Please. Listen: I don't know what I'll think of next, in the cellar. I've got Genet down there. And a complete de Sade. I'll reread them both, looking for increasingly complicated arabesques of sexual perversion. I may reappear with a whip. Wearing riding boots. Or dressed as a woman. Get out, darling. Run to the suburbs. Give my child a normal home. Go!

WIFE. Normal? Normal? (*She laughs uneasily.*) What is normal?

HUSBAND. You're normal, my love.

WIFE. Me? Oh, my God, how little do you know! (*Grimly.*) Sit down. I have a tale to tell-o.

HUSBAND. Nothing you could say . . .

WIFE. Sit down.

THE PROBLEM 15

HUSBAND. Nothing . . .
WIFE. I've known all along you were my dark lover!
HUSBAND. (*Sits down.*) You've known?
WIFE. From the beginning.
HUSBAND. But . . . how?
WIFE. Five years ago, when you announced to me that you had scheduled some evening classes, I became suspicious. And so when you left for the first class, I . . . followed you.
HUSBAND. Followed me?
WIFE. Yes. I followed my own husband. Followed you to that tacky little theatre-supply shop downtown where you bought your disguise. Followed you back here. Followed you into the cellar, hid behind the hot-water heater, watched you change into your poor, pathetic imitation of a Negro.
HUSBAND. You spied on me. . . .
WIFE. Yes, I spied on you, my darling. Furtively, suspiciously, like some aging matron. But when I saw what you were doing, when I understood that you were doing it for me, my heart went out to you. With a great rush of longing, I dashed back upstairs, eager to receive you, but at the same time terrified that you would see that I recognized you. Frantically, I dimmed the lights, to make things easier for both of us.
HUSBAND. I thought it was because you were romantic.
WIFE. I know you did, darling. And I let you think that. But no: it was simply so I wouldn't give myself away.
HUSBAND. You were acting? The whole time?
WIFE. Yes. Wasn't I good? Pretending that you were someone new and strange? I, I, who am no actress, improvising like a professional during that whole scene!
HUSBAND. (*Shaking his head.*) It's hard to believe. . . . You seemed so . . . excited!
WIFE. I was! I was terribly excited. I'll admit it. That strange, sly courtship, the banter, the give and

take, with all those peculiar racial overtones. I threw myself into it with a vengeance. But then . . . when you carried me into the bedroom . . . everything changed.

HUSBAND. What do you mean? I was a tiger!

WIFE. You were, darling. You were a tiger. But I wasn't.

HUSBAND. You said you loved me.

WIFE. I was only pretending. I really hated you.

HUSBAND. Hated me?

WIFE. Hated myself. It was awful. I felt so guilty. All my old sexual agonies were magnified, as it were, by a gallery of mirrors. I wanted at least to whimper, as I did normally, with you, when you were white, but now you were black, I had to stifle my own sighs. Worse: I had to pretend, to play, to *fake* the most authentic experience a woman can have! And all the time, I felt like a thing, an object, a creature without a soul, a poor, pathetic concubine in the arms of an Ethiopian potentate. And when you left—finally left—I just lay on the bed, arms folded across my breast, like a stone carving on my own tomb. It took every ounce of energy I could muster to rise and greet you at the door when you returned from your supposed class.

(*Pause.*)

HUSBAND. So. For the past five years you have been through hell.

WIFE. No. After that first ghastly evening, I suffered nothing.

HUSBAND. You mean, you grew accustomed . . .

WIFE. I mean, I wasn't there.

HUSBAND. You weren't there?

WIFE. No. I left the house right after you went into the cellar.

HUSBAND. But then who . . . was here . . . with me?

THE PROBLEM

WIFE. I got a substitute.

HUSBAND. I see.

WIFE. Oh, darling, try to understand. I simply could not endure another evening like that. The sham, the pretense—it revolted me. And yet I knew how much it meant to you! All the next day, I racked my brain, trying to figure out something which would satisfy us both. I took a long walk. I wandered all over town. Finally, about an hour before I was due home, I saw a woman. Who looked a little like me. Same hair, same height . . . roughly the same age. It was at least a chance. Before I really knew what I was doing, I approached her and asked her whether she'd like to sleep with a Negro. Naturally she said she would. And so now, for the past five years, this good woman has come here while you were in the cellar changing your clothes, and in the dim light, she has pretended to be me.

HUSBAND. I see.

WIFE. Do you hate me very much?

HUSBAND. No. I don't hate you. But I must say I'm somewhat . . . surprised.

WIFE. I suspected you would be.

HUSBAND. But what about that? (*Points to her stomach.*)

WIFE. (*Clutching her stomach.*) Ah, this . . .

HUSBAND. Yes. That. Whose is that?

WIFE. Now bear with me, darling. On these nights while you're in the cellar, and while this good woman is preparing herself for your return, I go off with a real Negro. There it is. In a nutshell. His Cadillac pulls up quietly in front. He flashes his lights. And I sneak out, and drive off with him into the black ghetto. There, on an old mattress, infested with lice, nibbled at by rats, we make love. Love which for the first time in my life I can give myself up to, since I feel that with him I am expiating not only my own guilt, but the guilt of all America.

HUSBAND. I see. And so he is the father of that.

WIFE. No.

HUSBAND. No?

WIFE. Somehow, even that relationship wasn't enough. Somehow, in the ghetto, with all that soul music pulsing around me, all that frustration, all that anger, I still felt as if I were not playing my part. So I betrayed my lover for his friend. And his friend for another. And so on and so forth, with Puerto Ricans, Mexican-Americans, and Indians on relief. Oh, darling, for the past five years, I've been offering myself as an ecstatic white sacrifice to anyone with an income of less than five thousand.

HUSBAND. And so the father is . . .

WIFE. Social Injustice, on a large and general scale.

HUSBAND. I see.

WIFE. And now you'll leave me, won't you?

HUSBAND. Me? Leave you now? (*Laughs peculiarly.*) I want to stay more than ever. (*Cleans his pipe carefully.*) What would you say . . . if I said . . . that everything you've told me . . . excites me?

WIFE. Excites you?

HUSBAND. Sets my blood boiling. Gives me strange, wild frissons of desire. . . . What would you say if I said that your ghetto experiences have lit a lurid light in my own loins?

WIFE. Really?

HUSBAND. (*Still cleaning his pipe; not looking at her.*) What would you say . . . if I said . . . that I suddenly want to exercise—how shall I put it?—a *droit de seigneur* on you? That I want to steal you from the peasants, and carry you into my bedroom, and ravage you with the reading lights going full blaze? (*Looks at her carefully.*) What would you say, if I said that? (*Pause; she looks at him coyly.*)

WIFE. I'd say . . . do it.

HUSBAND. Mmmm.

WIFE. (*Hastily.*) And let me add this: Let me add that a woman, too, is capable of weird desires. This is hard to say, but looking at you now, slouched in that chair, surrounded by your books and papers, I suddenly have the strange urge to experience the stale comforts of bourgeois married love. They say that Americans in Paris, surfeited by the rich food, yearn for the simple hamburger. So it is with me. For you. Tonight.

HUSBAND. (*Getting up slowly.*) Then . . .

WIFE. (*Backing away from him.*) But there's still this! (*Indicating her stomach.*) This problem!

HUSBAND. (*Moving toward her.*) That's no problem.

WIFE. No problem?

HUSBAND. That's just the premise to the problem. Now we've solved the problem we no longer need the premise.

WIFE. I fail to follow.

HUSBAND. That's just the starting mechanism. Now the motor's going, we no longer need the starter.

WIFE. (*Looking down at her stomach.*) Oh.

HUSBAND. (*Stalking her.*) That's not really a baby you have in there.

WIFE. (*Backing away.*) Not really a baby?

HUSBAND. No. That's a balloon you have in there.

WIFE. A balloon?

HUSBAND. A balloon. Or a bladder. Or an old beach ball.

WIFE. It's a baby. I'm practically positive.

HUSBAND. No, no. Look. I'll show you. (*Takes the pointed metal prong of his pipe cleaner and gives her a quick, neat jab in the stomach.*) Touché! (*There is a pop, and then a hissing sound. She slowly deflates. They both watch.*) You see? The problem was simply academic. (*Pause.*)

WIFE. (*Looking at him sheepishly.*) Aren't we awful?

HUSBAND. (*Going to his chair, closing his book, carefully marking the place.*) You started it.

WIFE. I know. It was my turn. You started the last one.

HUSBAND. (*Neatening his books and papers.*) Well, it's fun.

WIFE. Shouldn't we see a psychiatrist?

HUSBAND. (*Tapping out his pipe; putting his glasses in his glasses-case.*) Why? We're happy. (*Turns off his light. The stage is now lit only from a light off* L.)

WIFE. But we're so de*praved!* (*He looks at her, then throws back his head and gives a long Tarzan-like whoop; then he pounds his chest like a gorilla; she giggles.*) Quiet! You'll wake the children! (*He picks her up in his arms; she pummels him melodramatically; speaks in an English accent.*) No, Tarzan! White men do not take women by force! No, Tarzan! White men *court* their women! They are civilized, Tarzan. It's very complicated. Do you understand what I am saying? Com-pli-ca-ted. . . . Com-pli-. . . . (*She giggles and kicks as he carries her off* L.)

CURTAIN

GROUND PLAN:

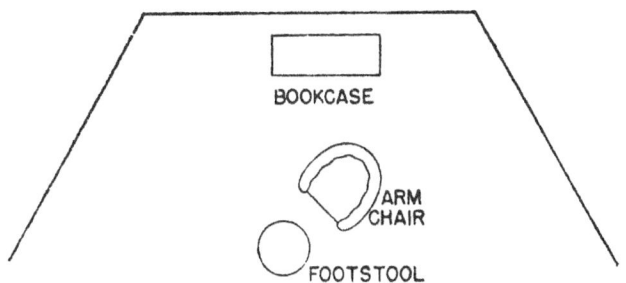

COSTUME PLOT

THE HUSBAND: Casual clothes, glasses.

THE WIFE: Maternity dress.

PROPERTY LIST

Several books
A pipe
A pencil and notebook
A metal pipe cleaner, sharp enough at one end to pop a balloon

www.ingramcontent.com/pod-product-compliance
Lightning Source LLC
Chambersburg PA
CBHW072023290426
44109CB00018B/2329